To dear Jan with much love from Susannah
Epiphany 1998

THE QUINTESSENTIAL GARDEN

⁓

First published in Great Britain in 1996
by The Windrush Press
Little Window, High Street,
Moreton-in-Marsh
Gloucestershire GL56 0LL

Telephone: 01608 652012
Fax: 01608 652125

British Library Cataloguing in Publication Data
A catalogue record for This book is available from
The British Library

ISBN 1 900624 00 1

Printed and bound in Slovenia
by Printing House Delo - Tiskarna
by arrangement with Korotan, Ljubljana

The QUINTESSENTIAL GARDEN

OR

PONDERING the GIANT SPINACH WEEVIL

JOCELYN WILD

THE WINDRUSH PRESS · GLOUCESTERSHIRE

FOR ROBIN

A NOTE on the history of BUMPKETTLE.

It was on their famous cycling Tour of Europe that The Bicycling Vikings, - or 'Bikings' came across an idyllic spot in The midst of the Droop marshes. They called the place 'Bumpkettle', - (Viking for 'the hill where we stopped for tea') and giving up their nomadic life Turned their ships into garden sheds and their bicycles into lawn mowers, and settled down to gardening. From these origens The people of Bumpkettle, and Lady Agrippa Deadnettle, its most illustrious inhabitant, are sprung.

WAITING FOR THE
MUSE: LADY AGRIPPA in the library
at Deadnettle Hall, at present
undergoing treatment for Death Watch Beetle by
Woodpecker. "It's cheaper than Rentokil," says Lady Agrippa,
who denies that the noise of 300 woodpeckers is a
slight distraction to her flow of inspiration.

A GRIPPA - LADY AGRIPPA DEADNETTLE, otherwise known as the
BLOOM OF BUMPKETTLE. Author of the outstanding BOOKY PRIZE
WINNER "THE SINKING OF THE BOTANIC," Lady Agrippa has recently
shaken the gardening world to the roots with her
ORGANIC GARDEN AIDS PROGRAMME,* designed to
revolutionise the entire concept of gardening. "It's
nothing but common sense, with a touch of genius,"
says Lady Agrippa, whose modesty has earned
her the title of the Shrinking Violet.

O.G.A.

LOOK FOR
THE SIGN!

* THE ORGANIC GARDEN AIDS BASIC KIT IS AVAILABLE FROM ALL GOOD GARDEN SHOPS,
CONSISTING OF A PACK CONTAINING: 2 HEDGEHOGS (for reproductive purposes, in
case of accident); 1 doz. SPIDERS, LARGE; 1 GROSS LADYBIRDS (not in same
envelope); 1 ANTEATER and 1 GOAT. AN ADDITIONAL ELEPHANT AND GIRAFFE
ALSO AVAILABLE AT SLIGHT EXTRA COST, as are ½ doz GUINEA PIGS, 1 RABBIT, 1 DONKEY
AND 4 SHEEP.

ANTEATER Useful for ridding the garden of unsightly ant hills, which it demolishes with its sharp claws, licking up the inhabitants by means of its long tongue.

ADVANTAGES: Sole food consists of ants, therefore requires no feeding

DISADVANTAGES: Sole food consists of ants, therefore when it has rid the garden of ants it will require feeding, which necessitates the reintroduction of ants into the garden.

ANTS in the garden,
a problem indeed, were it not for
our shaggy friend, the ANTEATER (right.)

ARTIST An important acquisition for the cultured gardener. Trouble free and requiring little attention, the ARTIST paints better if he is neglected and half starved.

THE LITTLE FLOWER GIRL
by Perseus Flot R.A.

BACKACHE

Also known in gardening terms as THE STOOPS, STEMDROOP, or in terminal cases, SNAP, - This condition is discernible by the tell-tale downward curve of the gardener.

EARLY ← STAGES

SECOND STAGE, The 'HALF HORSE-SHOE FOLD' ←

THE 'U-BEND,' OR FINAL STAGE, ↙ CHIN RESTING ON GROUND

GARDENER WITH STEMDROOP.

('SNAP' is not illustrated, because no live specimens available).

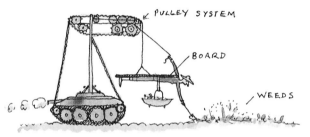

BACKACHE OR 'STEMDROOP' SUFFERER WEEDING WITH AID OF CONVENTIONAL BACKACHE PREVENTATIVE APPARATUS

IMPROVED BACKACHE PREVENTATIVE APPARATUS, LEAVING BOTH HANDS FREE FOR GREATER CONTROL OF WEEDS

BADGERS

– Nocturnal tresspassers particularly unwelcome on account of their passion for frantic and indiscriminate digging. DO NOT DESPAIR, – the erection of a BADGER BRIDGE will persuade these visitors – like The Angel of Death – To pass over your garden on The way To some one else's.

A BADGERBRIDGE IN OPERATION

BEANS, DWARF

Not a suitable crop To grow unless you are under 3 feet tall, and the cause of the painful condition known as 'Bean Neck'.

SUFFERER FROM 'BEAN NECK'.

LEFT, THE DWARF BEAN, KNOWN IN ENGLAND AS THE FRENCH BEAN, AND IN FRANCE AS THE ENGLISH BEAN, NEITHER NATION BEING WILLING TO CLAIM RESPONSIBILITY FOR THE INVENTION OF SUCH AN INCONVENIENT AND DISABLING VEGETABLE.

Note: An interesting theory for The term FRENCH BEAN being a corruption of TRENCH BEAN DERIVES FROM RESEARCH carried out by Professor PATÉ de PORC en CROÛTE for his article 'HARICOTS VERTS ET LA GUERRE,' in which he reveals that This legume was much grown by Troops in The FIRST WORLD WAR, its low growing habit making it admirably suited to TRENCH WARFARE.

A FRENCH SOLDIER PICKS BEANS IN THE MIDST OF A BOMBARDMENT

BEANS, RUNNER - The original symbol for the OLYMPIC GAMES.*

Pods, or BEANS from this versatile plant were used as batons in the first ever relay races. Participants in this sport came to be known as BEAN RUNNERS, and the beans subsequently grown for the purpose as RUNNER BEANS.

Bean

Interesting fact: Upon retirement the runner was known as a 'HAD BEANS,' which has since been corrupted to our modern expression, - a 'HAS BEEN.'

NOTE: RUNNER BEANS ARE NOT A SUITABLE CROP TO GROW UNLESS YOU ARE OVER 3 FEET TALL, or in the possession of a step ladder.

* The TORCH, a comparatively recent symbol for the Games is thought to have arrived on the athletic scene with a wave of Roman ice cream vendors, whose ice cream cornets became very popular with the spectators at the Games. Under the hot Aegean sun, however, the ice cream was in danger of instant melt down, and this soon gave rise to the familiar sight of Romans running very fast across the arena, cornets held aloft.

right: ROMAN ICE CREAM CORNET FROM WHICH THE FLAMING TORCH, THE PRESENT SYMBOL FOR THE OLYMPIC GAMES, EVOLVED.

BEAVERS - O.G.A. requiring ROUND THE CLOCK SUPERVISION, owing to its obsession for levelling every perpendicular object in the landscape, such as trees, telegraph poles, and in extreme cases, pylons. However, for certain tasks these willing little workers can be invaluable.

DEATH IN THE SHADE, - the scene at SEVEN OAKS (NOW SIX OAKS) HALL when working beavers TIMBER and TOPPLER escaped from their pen.

Above: CUTTING BEANSTICKS- well trained beavers working in a team.

BEES

Beneficial to the garden, though not always to the gardener.

A USEFUL DEVICE FOR
KEEPING BUMBLEBEES
OUT OF THE EARS WHILE
PICKING RASPBERRIES.

MISS EUREKA FLAX-BRITTLE IN THE
PETUNIA BED AT 'SPROCKETS',
ATTENDED BY A SWARM OF EARLY SPRING
HONEY BEES. "IT'S NOT THE STINGS I
MIND," SAYS MISS FLAX-BRITTLE, "IT'S
THE WAY THEY STEAM UP MY GLASSES."

ABOVE: LADY AGRIPPA, OTHERWISE KNOWN AS 'THE QUEEN BEE OF BUMPKETTLE',
PICTURED HERE WITH A SELECTION OF TASTEFULLY DESIGNED HOMES FOR BEES;
'COLDITZ', 'ARK ROYAL' AND 'ANNE HATHAWAY'S COTTAGE',
WHILE AT THE SAME TIME MODELLING THE 'SKEP TURBAN', - FOR
THE BEE KEEPER WHO LIKES TO KEEP 'AHEAD OF THINGS'

BIRDS

WAS ERE SUCH THRILL
AS THE TRILL
OF THE BLACKBIRD
HEARD
OR THE WARBLING THRUSH
ON YON BUSH ?

Ron Keates

THIMBLE JACCUZI FOR HUMMING BIRDS

ABOVE: CONVENTIONAL MODEL

BATH TIME FOR OUR FEATHERED FRIENDS :
However, every precaution should be taken to prevent the incursion of these creatures into the fruit and vegetable section of the garden. which is where they are usually headed after they have had their bath.

BOG GARDEN Extremely ancient form of garden. Gradually evolved into the SUNKEN GARDEN. No examples of these remain, - they have all sunk without trace.

THE CUTTING OF PAPYRUS FOR THE FIRST EDITION OF THE DROOP AND BUMPKETTLE DURGE, - IN THE BOG GARDENS OF LADY AGRIPPA'S ANCESTOR, - PRINCESS PTULIP PEDTAL * 100094 B.C.

SUNKEN PYRAMID

* INTERESTING HISTORICAL NOTE : HANDED DOWN TO LADY AGRIPPA WAS THE SECRET PASSWORD USED WHEN VISITING THE SEALED TOMBS OF ANCESTORS, - " Toot." ("Toot and come in.")

BOOKS ON GARDENING Some recommended reading for gardeners:

POISONOUS PLANTS, 15509 USES - by EWEL WRYTHE

LEARNING TO LOVE WEEDS - by Phyllis Twinkle

CATCHING WORMS, - by EARL E. BIRD

YOU CAN MAKE A ROCKERY FROM GALLSTONES - Y. Bother

IRISH LAND CRESS, - WHAT IS IT? - Ottalie Borin

THE MYSTERY OF THE SHRINKING HEAD GARDENER - by I. DUNNIT

I HAD A KIDNEY BEAN TRANSPLANT - by A. Fieldmouse

CACTUS BREEDING, - A HOBBY FOR THE SEDENTARY by Ivor Sorebottom

KNIT THIS CHARMING TEA COSY FROM BINDWEED - by Phyllis Twinkle

GARDENING IN A NUTSHELL - by Hazel Nut Weevil

AND - HOT OFF THE PRESSES! LADY AGRIPPA'S LATEST LITERARY OEUVRE, Winner of the BOOKY PRIZE: THE SINKING OF THE BOTANIC, - the story of the ill-fated ship, the BOTANIC, which sank off Bumpkettle Pier. Bound on a special scientific expedition in the cause of gardening, the BOTANIC sank without trace seconds after being launched with a bottle of Liquid Manure made to Lady Agrippa's secret recipe.

THE LAST GLIMPSE OF THE BOTANIC, A PHOTOGRAPH TAKEN SECONDS AFTER THE DISASTER. THE SHIP'S BAND, WITH RARE COURAGE, CONTINUED TO PLAY 'COME INTO THE GARDEN MAUD' AS THE WAVES SWALLOWED THEM UP.

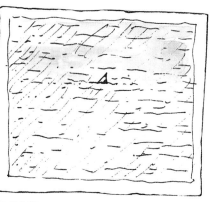

BOOKS ON GARDENING

CARNIVOROUS PLANTS - The ultimate in pest control if sited in a suitable spot. Will neatly dispose of all pests - including neighbours' cats and dogs and children, - and neighbours themselves when they come to look for them.

CAUTIOUS NOTE: CARNIVOROUS PLANTS if allowed to feed to excess may in their turn become a pest, disposing of all the gardener's (O.G.A.s) and indeed, in severe cases, the gardener himself.

REMAINS OF MISS MYRTLE THICKET whose disappearance is thought to be connected with the abnormal growth pattern of a CARNIVOROUS PLANT in her lettuce bed.

CATS Their usefulness in the garden in eliminating pests such as birds and mice is to some extent offset against certain undesirable habits of their own:

1.   2.   3.

CLOTHES LINES

No longer do these need to consist of two posts and a piece of string. Today's garment-hanging facilities are not only practical but aesthetic as well.

Some head-turning examples:

NEW WORLD · The 'BUCKING CLOTHES HORSE' (above) or 'WILD WEST ACTION LINE', in the form of a lassoo from realistic model cowboy on bucking bronco with additional terrified steer.

RUSTIC - 'GONE WITH THE WIND' (above), - reproduction windmill clothes whirler with internal staircase for access to hanging area.

MARINE : 'H.M.S. LAUNDRY' - a ship in full rigging, for the larger family

INDUSTRIAL (above) 'THE PYLON LINE' consisting of 2 PYLONS* connected

* FAKE, OR SURPLUS ELECTRICITY BOARD AS REQUIRED, BUT IN THE CASE OF THE LATTER CARE SHOULD BE TAKEN TO ENSURE THAT IT HAS BEEN DISCONNECTED FROM THE MAINS.

CLOTHES LINES (CONTD.)

ARTHURIAN (right)
particularly
suitable for
stately homes.

STEPPING STONES

OCEANIC (ABOVE) with added feature, - genuine Neptune's Trident CLOTHES PROP.

NATURE LOVER

'MONARCH OF THE GLEN' (above)

or, for those of a more
adventurous turn of
mind :
'SAFARI'
(right.)

And, for single items, -
the handy sized
'CLASSICAL' (above)

DEATH IN THE GARDEN This need not cause inconvenience. Simply place the deceased on the compost heap, adding a light covering of leaves, cabbage stalks etc., and leave for six months.

DIGGING For painless digging without lifting a finger,- (if you use your finger. It is more common to use a spade), try any of the following:

1. THE HISTORICAL METHOD: Inform the local ARCHEOLOGICAL SOCIETY that you have discovered traces of buried treasure in your garden. The digging will be thorough.

Note: KEEP AN EYE ON PROCEEDINGS IN CASE THEY DO FIND ANYTHING, SO THAT YOU CAN CLAIM IT.

2. THE HUNGRY MOLE METHOD: Sprinkle EARTHWORMS evenly over the area to be dug. MOLES will immediately appear from nowhere in search of the worms, at the same time throwing up the soil in little mounds. This method makes for an unusual landscaped effect.

Right: Result of the HUNGRY MOLE METHOD OF DIGGING

ADULT MOLE AND MOLECULE (young mole)

3. THE TUSKER PLOUGH: consisting simply of a pair of trained Pachioderms (MAMMOTHS preferable, if available, but elephants will do, and at a pinch, WARTHOGS) who simply turn over the sod with their tusks.

A HEART-WARMING SIGHT,-
TRADITIONAL PLOUGHING
by Pachioderm

NB DIGGING BY BADGER IS <u>NOT</u> RECOMMENDED.

left,- 'Gibberings,' - home for confused gardeners, after a night of digging by badgers. It was said they were attracted by half a mars Bar accidentally dropped in a hydrangea bush.

DISASTERS

Look on the bright side. The skilful gardener will turn setbacks to advantage:

<u>COWS</u> in the garden, can be a welcome arrival, for instance when visiting relations linger too long

or when you are short of milk.

<u>THAT BYPASS</u> routed through your strawberry patch <u>could</u> be heaven sent:

<u>THE EARTHQUAKE</u> : A conversation piece for admiring visitors, as are VOLCANOES, HURRICANES, TYPHOONS AND TIDALWAVES (see SPECIAL EFFECTS)

<u>WAR</u> can be turned to some profit. Treat in the same way as BYPASS (above) As Lady AGRIPPA's Swiss Ancestor, FRÄU HILDEBAG remarked when Hannibal's elephants on their historic march over the Alps ran amok through her 5000 year old MEDLAR GROVE:

"VELL, EET SAVES PEEKING ZEM, UND I NEVER DEED LIKE MEDLARS ANYVAY." (who does?)

DISEASES IT IS ADVISABLE NOT TO COME INTO THE GARDEN IF YOU ARE DISEASED

Common DISEASES to which gardeners are prone include:

SPLITTING

WILT

BLACK SPOT

CRINKLE

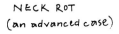

NECK ROT
(an advanced case)

GREY MOULD

REVERSION

BROWN ROT

BLACK LEG

MOSAIC

CLUB ROOT

DIE BACK

BAD NEWS: As there is NO CURE for these ailments The sufferer must prepare to meet The Great Gardener in the Sky.

NOTE: VULTURES hovering over the cabbages are a tell tale sign that something is amiss. (vultures do not eat cabbages, but they do eat dead gardeners.) For what to do in this case see: DEATH IN THE GARDEN.

DOGS Not generally regarded as a pest in the garden, except for:

1.   2.

and a certain amount of wear and tear on the not so hardy annuals when looking for its ball.

DOGS IN EXCESS, (that is, hounds, packs of wolves etc.) may be swiftly diverted from your garden by judicious sprinkling of special 'ESSENCE of CAT' drops * on the path leading to your neighbour's garden.

*AVAILABLE FROM YOUR LOCAL PERFUMERIE.

DUNG   The importance of this substance was first realised by the Chinese Emperor Pong Ho of the ancient DUNG DYNASTY. Indeed, it came to be considered such a precious commodity that one vase of YIN DUNG (there was also YAN DUNG and YON DUNG) was worth 10028 dung YEN.

AN EARLY DUNG VASE

A DUNG MOO

ABOVE: DUNG WAS GATHERED BY CHINESE MAIDENS AT SPECIAL DUNG CEREMONIES.

LEFT: RECEPTACLE FOR THE INFUSION OF 'DUNG TEA', AN ANCIENT CHINESE CURE FOR THE SPORTING DISABILITY KNOWN AS 'PING PONG CHIN' (the Chinese equivalent of 'Tennis Elbow')

ELEPHANTS IN THE GARDEN

O.G.A. Not enough can be said on this important Topic. The largest of the ORGANIC GARDEN AIDS, the ELEPHANT is of incalculable use to the gardener. Affectionate companion as well as useful aid, it is an ideal gift for a loved one. However, EXTREME CARE is needed To ensure that this **O.G.A** has previously been Trained, as examples wild from the jungle have occasionally been imported, with tragic consequences for both garden and gardener.

KEEP YOUR LAWN TRIM with this simple ROLLING / SPIKING device consisting of an ELEPHANT (or several if you have a large lawn) fitted with special spike-soled sandals* and rolling a tree trunk along.

* ORIGINALLY WORN TO GET A GRIP ON THE ICE WHEN CROSSING THE ALPS.

MEDLARS

NOTE:
THE 'HANNIBAL'S HOBBYHORSE' ROLLER/SPIKER (above) is UNSUITABLE FOR SLOPING LAWNS, OWING TO THE UNPREDICTABILITY OF THE MECHANISM.

Below: An elephant is also invaluable for GATHERING IN THE CIDER APPLES.

ARMOUR.

NOTE: EXPERIMENTS ARE CURRENTLY UNDER WAY TO CROSS AN ELEPHANT WITH A GIANT ARMADILLO IN AN EFFORT TO PRODUCE THE IDEAL **O.G.A** FOR THIS TASK.

ELEPHANTS (CONTINUED)

GARDENER'S DELIGHT - Just one of 1001 uses for your organic horticultural aid, - THE ELEPHANT:

GALLANT AND OBLIGING, THE ELEPHANT IS ALSO USEFUL FOR CARRYING DECK CHAIRS.

CARE OF YOUR ELEPHANT: The medium sized elephant requires daily nourishment as follows:

ONE LARGE TREE (or Two small)

2 CWT BOILED RICE (or in Scotland one bath full of porridge NOT Too hot)

500 GALLONS WATER.

NOTE: IT IS ADVISABLE TO GIVE IT A DAILY RUB WITH BABY OIL
TO GUARD AGAINST CHILBLAINS (above)
SEE "CARING FOR YOUR ELEPHANT," - A MINISTRY OF HORTICULTURE
LEAFLET (available from Bumpkettle General Post Office)

FERTILIZER

A valuable product for the garden, accidentally discovered by a district nurse — LIZA FERTINGALE, who was living in the ALPS when Hannibal marched through with his elephants. Well known throughout history as the 'LADY OF THE LUMP' (for she had in fact a large lump or CARBUNCLE over her right eyebrow) LIZA FERTINGALE rose to fame during a severe epidemic of SWISS MEASLES which put the whole of HANNIBAL'S army in bed. Filled with healing zeal, The Lady of the Lump called at the barracks and administered doses of a special homeopathic medicine made to an ancient Swiss recipe, the ingredients consisting mainly of goat cheese, stewed medlars, and eidelweiss. It proved a miracle cure, — the invalids no matter how ill leapt out of bed the instant they saw (or rather smelled) her coming with her proffered medicament.

Later, applied to a row of SWISS CHARD, it was discovered that the plants shot up 3 feet in a single day, — with shock, scientists said.

RECOVERING FROM A DEBILITATING BOUT OF SWISS MEASLES, HANNIBAL DECLINES AN OFFER OF DISTRICT NURSE LIZA FERTINGALE'S SPECIAL MEDICINE, — WHILE ATTEMPTING TO CONFER ON HER THE CROIX DE GUERRE FOR SERVICES RENDERED.

FLOATING GARDENS

Egyptian waterborne pleasure garden mounted on crocodiles. A popular craft for picnics on The Nile,— hense The term "a movable feast."

THE BARGE SHE SAT IN... QUEEN COLLYDOTRA TAKES REFRESHMENT ABOARD HER FLOATING GARDEN ON THE NILE. THE SYMBOLS DENOTE THAT A SEDATIVE HAS BEEN ADMINISTERED,— TO PREVENT EGYPT'S QUEEN FROM BECOMING A MOVABLE FEAST FOR THE CROCODILES.

FLYING GARDENS

Ancient Arabian form of horticulture. Specially developed for desert conditions, the FLYING GARDEN could be conveniently steered towards The nearest rain cloud for watering.

Above:
WATERING TIME FOR SHEIK ALI OOP'S FLYING GARDEN IN THE ARABIAN DESERT

GARDEN FURNITURE

Designs are various, including the notable:

1. CAMOUFLAGE GARDEN TABLE AND CHAIR SET, (below) designed to blend into the surroundings.

2. The NATURE LOVER'S LOOKOUT POST, (right) consisting of a reproduction hollow tree with one-person seating capacity, including handy shelf for nature notes or coffee cup.

HIDDEN ENTRANCE SO AS TO DECEIVE WILD LIFE

AND

O.G.A.

Of remarkable interest is the LATEST LINE in garden furniture, while being at the same time AS OLD AS THE HILLS, -

3. the TORTOISE SUITE, - unusual rot-proof mobile garden seating (GIANT TORTOISES ONLY, unless you are a dwarf.) IDEAL for GARDEN PARTIES, you need never get bored having to sit next to someone you don't like, for sooner or later your seat will wander away. Can be controlled by a simple cabbage lure. (see below)

NOTE: CARE IS NEEDED WHEN HANDLING YOUR MOBILE GARDEN SEATING IN THE MATING SEASON.

GARDEN PARTIES Usually held for friends, on the assumption that enemies are likely to be prejudicial to the garden. For something completely different try:

1. A PORRIDGE PARTY, - (an old Scottish tradition). Nothing could be more enchanting on a frosty morning in mid-January. Delight your friends by asking them, - they'll love you for it. <u>ECONOMICAL</u>!!! <u>OR</u> how about:

2. A RAIN DANCE, - fashionable in England, where they are 100% effective. <u>OR</u>, more energetic:

3. A DUNG FLING! A cross between a barn dance and an old fashioned quilting bee. Get your dung flung all over the garden in a Trice, according to the old addage 'MANY HANDS - (Forks are advisable in this case) - MAKE LIGHT WORK'.

ABOVE: PREPARING FOR THE PORRIDGE PARTY, - THE QUAINT OLD SCOTTISH WAY OF MAKING MERRY.

GARDEN SHEDS CAN be unsightly, but tasteful designs are available, to blend in with the surroundings.

LEFT: SHED IN THE GUISE OF A CASTLE.

RIGHT: SHED DESIGNED AS A BUSH (free standing) or for slotting into the hedge so as not to show at all (below)

INVISIBLE SHED IN THIS HEDGE

Also come disguised as COMPOST HEAP, and COMPOST HEAP disguised as GARDEN SHED.

GRAVES

A sprinkling of these add an individual Touch to the garden where a sombre note is required. The selection ranges from MEMORIALS To loved ones, for The spacious garden, to the discreet URN (with or without ashes/bones) for the small garden. For The extra spacious garden, - a MAUSOLEUM, - perhaps a life-size replica of the TAJ MAHAL, or, more unusual, The TOMB OF THE UNKNOWN GARDENER, with its moving sculpture of Fork, Spade and Trowel that says it all.

MODEST BUT MOVING, - A FUNEREAL URN LENDS A SOMBRE NOTE TO THE GARDEN (above).

PATHETIC TOUCH: GRAVES OF PETS, - And in certain circumstances graves of pets' victims, - will bring a Tear To the eye

TRAGICALLY IMPOSING - EVEN THE STONIEST HEART WILL MELT WHEN THIS GRAND MONUMENT, SET IN A GROVE OF WEEPING WILLOWS, HOVES INTO VIEW.

HA·HA

Horticultural device, consisting of a ditch* dug round the garden to prevent incursions from unwelcome visitors. Not effective against KANGAROOS, ELEPHANTS, BABOONS CARRYING LADDERS, SNAKES OR LOCUSTS, to name but a few. So not very effective at all, in fact.

MEDLARS

Fence

HA·HA →

Above: HIGH SPIRITED ELEPHANTS
WELCOME THE CHALLENGE OF A HA·HA.

* A smaller version of this horticultural device, the MINI·HA·HA, was in use in the 19th century in North America. The poet LONGFELLOW encountered one when he went out shooting the rapids (now a protected species,) in the rainy season. There was a cloudburst at the time, which caused severe flooding, or high water, — 'Hiawatha' in the local tongue. In order to cross the Hiawatha he was obliged to jump a Mini·ha·ha, an experience which gave rise to these memorable lines, written to his parents, and later found at the bottom of the ditch:

> ... I am in a spot of bother,
> Dearest Father and Mama·ha,
> For to cross the Hiawatha
> I must jump this Mini·haha.
>
> Now I'm soaked and getting wetter
> - This has really gone too fa·ha, -
> And I've dropped my blooming letter
> In the blasted Mini·ha·ha..."

LONGFELLOW'S HAT, WHICH ALSO
DOUBLED AS INKWELL, WITH
QUILL ATTACHED.

HANGING GARDENS

Referred to in the Scriptures, these were a hobby of KING NEBUCHADNEZZAR's, whose other preoccupation was his immaculate lawn (see Lawns). The phrase really referred to the HANGING GARDENERS of Babylon, who were suspended by the ankles, cultivating the rough cliffs that overlooked the WATERS of BABYLON.

GARDENER CASUALTY

HANNIBAL

Responsible for introducing ELEPHANTS to gardening, - accidentally, while traversing the Alps. They were meant to march along the road, but preferred a more circuitous route through the orchards and vegetable gardens of the local inhabitants.

HANNIBAL'S PIPE

HEDGEHOGS

A useful aid to the gardener, particularly at gooseberry picking time, and as a mud brush for dirty boots. But care must be taken not to step on them while picking peas, watering etc., when these creatures have a tendancy to be just where they are least expected. Extremely accident-prone.

right:
Hedgehog revolving mudscraper.

NOTE: it is advisable to give the hedgehog a saucer of milk after you have used it, or the next time it may not cooperate.

HEDGE TRIMMING.

O.G.A. No need to cry when hedgetrimming Time comes round again, for the FULLY ADJUSTABLE ANIMATED HEDGE TROLLEY has been specially developed to deal with this problem. Combining revolutionary simplicity with brilliant subtlety, this device will not only trim _any_ hedge including holly and bramble, but will actually tell you when to move on. Consisting of a wheeled platform to which is affixed a DONKEY, a GOAT and a RABBIT, there is also a special low filling available for a TORTOISE if necessary. (But the speed must be adjusted in the case of the latter, which might occasion much noise, owing to the impatience of the others.)

THE ANIMATED HEDGE TROLLEY IN ACTION

HIGH *
MIDDLING
LOW
EXTRA LOW.

* for exceptionally high hedges a giraffe may also be added, see below.

For <u>extra tall</u> hedges the handy, or rather necky piece of equipment is the GIRAFFE.

A GIRAFFE REACHES THE PARTS OTHER **O.G.As** CANNOT REACH.

HONOURS FOR GARDENING

The R.H.C. (Royal Horticultural Corps) achieved fame during the First World War when they got the H.U.M.P. that coveted award (for HEROIC UNDERTAKINGS MINDLESS of PERIL) On arrival at the front line at midnight they misinterpreted the order "GET DUG IN" as "GET DIGGIN'" with the result that by daylight the whole battlefield had been thoroughly dug over. The enemy, alarmed at what they took to be some new and deadly form of warfare evacuated their trenches in an instant, thus affording the Allies a glorious gain of 12 yards 2 feet and 7¼ inches without a shot being fired.

The highest PEACETIME HONOUR ever awarded was the M.U.G. - 'Medal for Useful Gardening,' - which went to one Amos THWARTFETTLE (1811 - 1916) who successfully raised 35 cucumbers, 4 yards of mustard and cress, and a dozen parsnips on a tightrope garden stretched across the Victoria Falls.

EMBODIMENT OF THE COLONIAL SPIRIT - AMOS THWARTFETTLE CULTIVATES HIS TIGHTROPE GARDEN ACROSS THE VICTORIA FALLS IN THE FACE OF CONSIDERABLE DANGER

ICE PLANTS

Found in areas of frozen waste, such as the North Pole, where the ice produced is harvested for export.

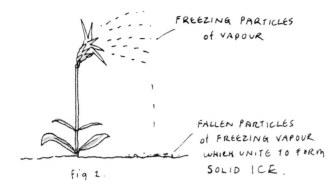

FREEZING PARTICLES of VAPOUR

FALLEN PARTICLES of FREEZING VAPOUR WHICH UNITE TO FORM SOLID ICE.

Fig 1.

PRODUCING ICE FROM THE ICE PLANT

ICE

Fig 2.
ESKIMOS HARVESTING ICE.

RIGHT: 'BACK TO BASICS' — THE IMPOSING SCULPTURE IN PURE ARCTIC ICE, SPECIALLY COMMISSIONED FOR THE B.H.S., (Bumpkettle Horticultural Society) ANNUAL DINNER AND DANCE. THE ROOM TEMPERATURE HAS BEEN SET AT -40% CENTIGRADE, TO PREVENT A REPETITION OF THE FREAK ACCIDENT THAT OCCURRED THE PREVIOUS YEAR, WHEN THE CHAIRMAN AND HIS WIFE WERE TRAGICALLY CRUSHED BY A FALLING INDEX FINGER, (The sculpture that year was entitled 'BUMPKETTLE HORTICULTURE NEEDS YOU!') WHILE THEY WERE DANCING THE FOX TROT.

INDIA BRITANNICA GARDENS

INDIA BRITANNICA GARDENS – An invention of the thirteenth viceroy, LORD DAWDLEFORTH. These small compact gardens, carried on the backs of elephants, were ingeniously designed to fit together, the elephants standing in close proximity in the manner of a living jigsaw puzzle. Upon the area so formed, – the size of Hyde Park or greater, – The viceroy and his retinue roamed at will, indulging in character building sports such as polo or big game hunting.

PROTECTION FROM THE SUN OR THE MONSOON RAIN AS REQUIRED. The elephant is also trained to suck up moisture from small ponds and water the garden on its back.

Above:
LORD DAWDLEFORTH, VICEROY OF INDIA, ORDERS A WHISKY AND SODA AFTER A HARD DAY'S WORK TOURING THE PROVINCES.
NOTE THE ELEPHANTS FOOTBRACELETS TO PREVENT SERPENTS FROM ALIGHTING UP ITS LEGS AND SHARING EDEN'S DELIGHTS WITH THE VICEROY.

JEWELLERY - What the fashion-conscious gardener is wearing:

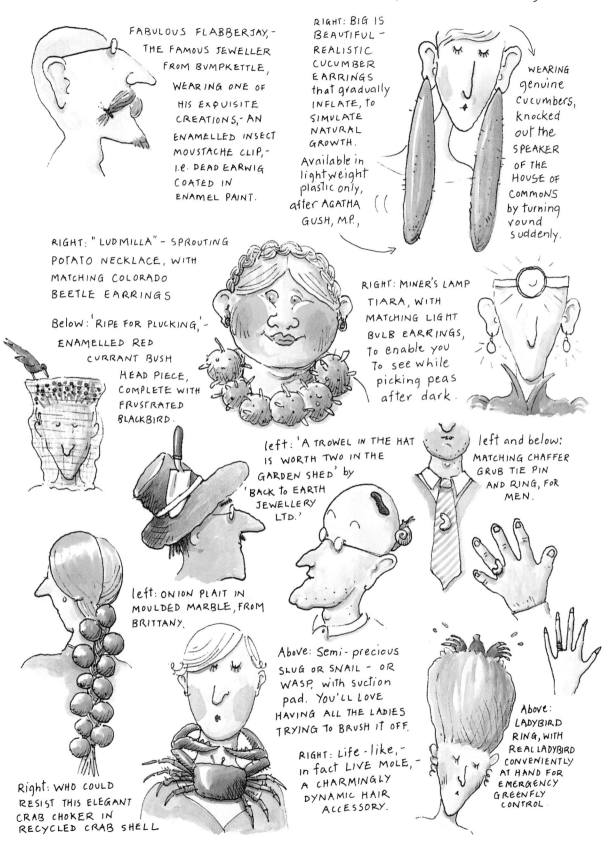

FABULOUS FLABBERJAY, - THE FAMOUS JEWELLER FROM BUMPKETTLE, WEARING ONE OF HIS EXQUISITE CREATIONS, - AN ENAMELLED INSECT MOUSTACHE CLIP, - I.e. DEAD EARWIG COATED IN ENAMEL PAINT.

RIGHT: BIG IS BEAUTIFUL - REALISTIC CUCUMBER EARRINGS that gradually INFLATE, TO SIMULATE NATURAL GROWTH. Available in lightweight plastic only, after AGATHA GUSH, M.P.,

WEARING genuine Cucumbers, knocked out the SPEAKER OF THE HOUSE OF COMMONS by turning round suddenly.

RIGHT: "LUDMILLA" - SPROUTING POTATO NECKLACE, WITH MATCHING COLORADO BEETLE EARRINGS

Below: 'RIPE FOR PLUCKING,' - ENAMELLED RED CURRANT BUSH HEAD PIECE, COMPLETE WITH FRUSTRATED BLACKBIRD.

RIGHT: MINER'S LAMP TIARA, WITH MATCHING LIGHT BULB EARRINGS, To enable you To see while picking peas after dark.

left: 'A TROWEL IN THE HAT IS WORTH TWO IN THE GARDEN SHED' by 'BACK TO EARTH JEWELLERY LTD.'

left and below: MATCHING CHAFFER GRUB TIE PIN AND RING, FOR MEN.

left: ONION PLAIT IN MOULDED MARBLE, FROM BRITTANY.

Above: Semi- precious SLUG OR SNAIL - OR WASP, with suction pad. You'LL LOVE HAVING ALL THE LADIES TRYING TO BRUSH IT OFF.

RIGHT: Life-like, - in fact LIVE MOLE, - A CHARMINGLY DYNAMIC HAIR ACCESSORY.

Above: LADYBIRD RING, WITH REAL LADYBIRD CONVENIENTLY AT HAND FOR EMERGENCY GREENFLY CONTROL.

Right: WHO COULD RESIST THIS ELEGANT CRAB CHOKER IN RECYCLED CRAB SHELL

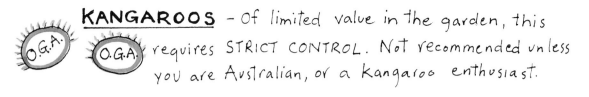

KANGAROOS - Of limited value in the garden, this requires STRICT CONTROL. Not recommended unless you are Australian, or a kangaroo enthusiast.

1.

2.

Above: THE USES OF THE KANGAROO ARE CONSIDERABLY OFFSET BY ITS ERRATIC BEHAVIOUR.

KNOT GARDENS - A horticultural fad in Elizabethan times. Not worth mentioning, except for an interesting recent discovery:

WOT NOTTE

WEN is YE GARDEN
NOTTE YE GARDEN?

ANSER —
WEN IT IS YE
KNOTTE GARDEN
W.R.

PLAYFUL RIDDLE PENNED BY
SIR WALTER RALEIGH TO
AN UNKNOWN LADY.
IT IS THOUGHT HE WAS
BETTER AT GARDENING
THAN HE WAS AT
SPELLING.

left — a delightful example of Elizabethan wit, this fragment was found in a false toe cap in Sir Walter Raleigh's gardening boot.

NOW IN BUMPKETTLE MUSEUM.

LADYBIRDS

These creatures, distantly related to The TORTOISE, are an invaluable aid in the garden, doing battle, in their own tiny fashion, with noxious GREENFLY, WHITEFLY and BLACKFLY, which damage plants.

PURE TORTOISE

PURE LADYBIRD

LADYTOISE
(LADYBIRD X
with TORTOISE)

TORBIRD
(TORTOISE X with
LADYBIRD)

The Modern method of distributing LADYBIRDS is by A HANDY DISPENSER (adjustable as required, depending on whether They are fat ladybirds or thin ladybirds) for squirting them on infested plants. (see below)

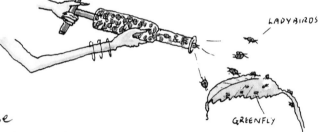

LADYBIRDS

GREENFLY

NOTE: The reader's interest may be accorded To the recent Tragic case of a short sighted gardening enthusiast who boiled $\frac{1}{2}$ lb of LADYBIRDS for soup in The mistaken assumption that The small round orange Things were lentils. (The soup was delicious, claimed The lady, interviewed later.) The SOCIETY for the PROTECTION OF LADYBIRDS AND THINGS (S.P.L.A.T.) dropped The case against her when it was revealed That The incident Took place at night and There was no Tell Tale movement owing To The little creatures all being sound asleep. The case To decide whether or not They had been DRUGGED is still pending.

LAWN   An area of grass which requires mowing. Fortunately LADY AGRIPPA has been researching some ALTERNATIVE LAWN MOWERS, which will considerably lighten This burdensome Task:

1. The Charmingly rustic BAA MOW, consisting of a team of hungry sheep yoked Together for precision steering. No fumes! No noise! (apart from the occasional baa), no Trouble with starting! This little outfit moves off in an instant, eager to do The Task.

NOTE: SKILFUL STEERING IS ESSENTIAL

NOTE: THE LEANER THE SHEEP, THE FASTER THE MOWING

THE BAA MOW IN ACTION.

2. Less restful, but faster and independantly powered:

The YAP MOW, a machine pulled by dog chasing cat chasing mouse (which is not chasing anything but running for its life.) Care must be taken To see That none of the participants are actually able to reach the one in front or instant breakdown will occur.

The YAP MOW de luxe comes with attachable little trailer full of guinea pigs, who Turn grass mowings, in due time, into handy no-mess manure in The form of pellets which can be sprinkled round the garden. (see below)

THE YAP MOW de luxe.

OTHER LAWN IMPLEMENTS:

1. The H.T.N. ('HOMAGE TO NEBUCHADNEZZAR'), is the ideal combined LAWN ROLLER / SPIKER. Easily adaptable from an ordinary bicycle, The H.T.N. is noiseless, - The only sounds are the squeaks of the occasional mole being pricked by the cactus spikes. The GIANT CACTI ROLLERS are conveniently refillable, obtainable by post from:

NOMADIC TRIBES ENTERPRISES INC. *
GOBI DESERT
MONGOLIA.

BELOW: THE H.T.N. (**HOMAGE TO NEBUCHADNEZZAR**) COMBINED ROLLER/SPIKER will do a power of good to your lawn.

* NOTE: AS THE NOMADIC TRIBES ARE nomadic, some time may elapse before the postman manages to locate them so allow several years for your order.

INTERESTING ARTISTIC NOTE: It is not generally known that French lawns consist not of grass but of herbs; viz. that famous painting by MAYONNAISE entitled DEJEUNER SUR L'HERBE, which translated is found to mean 'LUNCH ON THE HERB', - The herb in this case being CATMINT, which accounts for the number of cats who have appeared on the scene. The birds who have come for the crumbs, are not now visible in this painting, - having in their turn become dejeuner pour les chats.

'DEJEUNER SUR L'HERBE' (French)
or 'LUNCH ON THE CATMINT,' by MAYONNAISE.

MINIATURE GARDENS

Ideal for the small gardener, or for misers. Also for gardeners on the move, — TRAMPS, CRIMINALS ON THE RUN, AIRLINE PILOTS, LONG DISTANCE RUNNERS etc.

special bell harness attachment to which is affixed shaft of light trolley containing miniature garden

'THE LONGLINESS OF THE LONG DISTANCE RUNNER'... but not when he can take his miniature garden with him (above.)

A method of gardening much favoured by the busy famous. Evil Knieval and Dr. Livingstone were both enthusiastic patrons of HORTICULTURE IN MINIATURE.

ON HIS EPIC TREK THROUGH THE RAIN FORESTS OF EQUATORIAL AFRICA DR. LIVINGSTONE PAUSES TO PRUNE A WEEPING WILLOW IN HIS MINIATURE GARDEN

MINIATURE GARDENS (CONTINUED)

Accompanied by his miniature garden (in side car) Evil Knieval astonishes the sporting world with another record jump in the local car park at Rusty Springs, South Dakota

Right: Before the invention of smelling salts, unpleasant odours were counteracted by a few strongly perfumed herbs grown in a special false gusset in a lady's gown.

For the practical garden lover, the MINIATURE GARDEN is ideal for the person going on holiday (particularly those who do not trust their neighbours to water their plants), or merely for short visits to friends (below)

Hand operated watering device

above: REFRESHMENT TIME FOR YOUR MINIATURE GARDEN NEED NOT INTERRUPT THE FLOW OF CONVERSATION

NEBUCHADNEZZAR

NEBUCHADNEZZAR Babylonian king fond of gardening (see Hanging Gardens of Babylon) and in particular of HIS LAWN. A perfectionist, he preferred to get down on his hands and knees and bite off the blades of grass with his own teeth rather than trust it to the Royal mowing machine. Eventually died a tragic and violent death, devoured by a leopard who mistook the royal lawn cropper for a domestic goat.

THE ROYAL MOWING MACHINE, POWERED BY SLAVES

KING NEBUCHADNEZZAR, - ROYAL HERBIVORE

NEIGHBOURS (see PESTS)

NETS A so called 'protection' for fruit and vegetables in the garden, nets are in reality the opposite*, being a flagrant signal to birds, rabbits, squirrels etc. that your produce is at last ripe and ready for eating. AVOID netting your produce, - keep the pests waiting. Sooner or later your neighbour will net his fruit etc., and the creatures will eagerly flock to his crop, leaving yours untouched.

* PESTS FIND NO DIFFICULTY IN WRIGGLING, SQUEEZING OR BITING THEIR WAY UNDER ANY NET, - INDEED, THEY ENJOY THE CHALLENGE.

AFFIXING THE GARDEN NET REQUIRES SKILL, - OR THIS CAN HAPPEN

right: Raspberry 'Astringent' - The 'Green Raspberry,' a useful little berry which never ripens, thus outwitting even the most patient blackbird. (the juice is said to make excellent disinfectant fluid for stables)

NURSERY GARDENS
Where the new crop of young gardeners are brought up in the way of gardening, in special HOT HOUSES.

Taught to handle a trowel at an early age ———

EACH NURSERY has its special potting sheds

Precautions taken to prevent DAMPING OFF

A Top dressing Applied

DOUBLE DIGGING

Tendrils or 'suckers' are taken in charge by the adult or 'BIG BUD' of the Nursery.

BEDDING OUT

Female (Fertilization carried out by bees)

TENDER YOUNG SPROUT

HALF-HARDY ANNUAL

HARDY PERENNIALS

PERENNIAL GOING TO SEED

ORNAMENTS IN THE GARDEN Some unusual and aesthetic

ornaments with which to beautify your garden:

A SACRIFICIAL ALTAR which doubles as a BARBECUE. Comes with
matching OUTDOOR PULPIT, - on wheels for mobility, so that your audience
cannot slink away.

SPREADING THE WORD, -
THE MATCHING
GENUINE OLD TESTAMENT
SACRIFICIAL ALTAR
BARBECUE (left) and
MOBILE OUTDOOR PULPIT
ARE A GODSEND FOR
MISSIONARIES,
JEHOVAH'S WITNESSES,
AND ENVIRONMENTAL
CAMPAIGNERS.

← FIRE

FOR THE EDUCATED GARDENER, -
THAT CLASSICAL TOUCH:
BATTERED GREEK WARRIOR,
IN STONE, PLUS GENUINE
ELGIN MARBLE, (left)

URNS, TEMPLES, STATUES, STEPS AND GROTTOES in various materials
according to desire, as knocked about as possible, for that authentic look.
ALSO: 'STONE' ornaments specially fashioned in PAPER by the ancient
Japanese craft of ORIGAMI, -(below), for gardens prone to EARTHQUAKES.

TAKING TEA IN A
TOKYO GARDEN FITTED
WITH PAPER ORNAMENTS,
DURING AN EARTHQUAKE.

ORNAMENTAL FOUNTAINS, CASCADES, WATERFALLS, ETC.

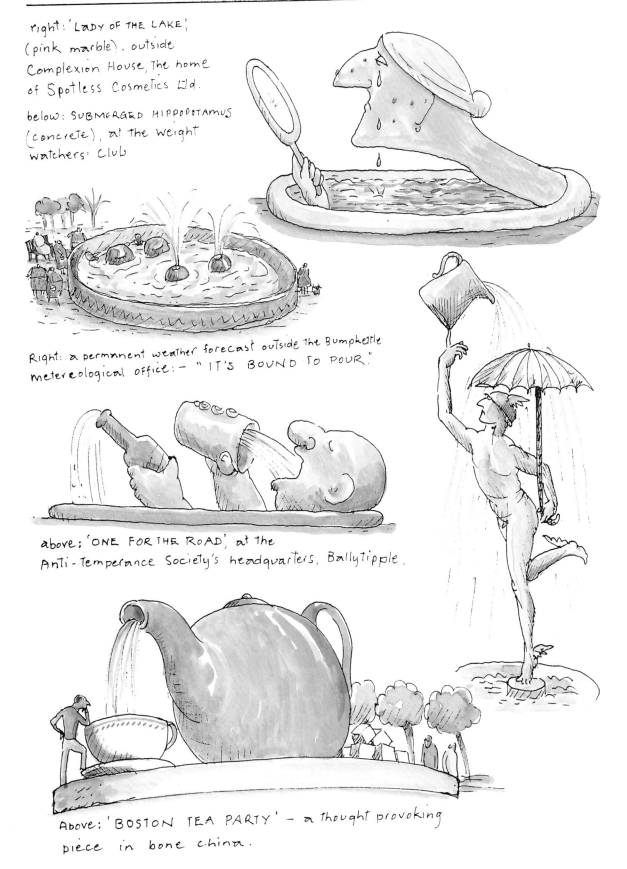

right: 'LADY OF THE LAKE',
(pink marble), outside
Complexion House, The home
of Spotless Cosmetics Ltd.

below: SUBMERGED HIPPOPOTAMUS
(concrete), at the Weight
watchers' Club

Right: a permanent weather forecast outside the Bumpkettle
metereological office:— "IT'S BOUND TO POUR."

above: 'ONE FOR THE ROAD', at the
Anti-Temperance Society's headquarters, Ballytipple.

Above: 'BOSTON TEA PARTY' — a thought provoking
piece in bone china.

OTHER PEOPLE'S GARDENS

1. A RAILWAY GARDEN AT BUMPKETTLE JUNCTION

BELOW:
MISS IVY SMING DEMONSTRATES
THE SPRING-APART MECHANISM
IN HER CHARMING GARDEN AT
BUMPKETTLE EAST.

Toot! Toot!

1. TRAIN APPROACHES

2. EDEN DIVIDED

2 A SEASIDE GARDEN WITH A DIFFERENCE:
Mr. Randolf Darning, light house keeper
at Aaddlestone Rock, disbuds his gloxinias
while his daughter Miss GREASE DARNING
braves gigantic seas to bring her father
his Lunchtime bottle of stout and
cheese and pickle sandwiches

3 SUBTERRANEAN DELIGHT
below The BUSY STREETS OF PARIS.

left. MONSIEUR SEWERAT WHO LIVES
in The underground drainage system
of Paris and has never seen the light of
day since he was 5 years old,
with his superb collection of algae.

OTHER PEOPLE'S GARDENS (CONTINUED)

4. A VERTICLE PARADISE ON THE WHITE CLIFFS OF BUMPKETTLE

LORD AND LADY GRAPPLINGHOOKS - AWASH (pronounced GOSH) with their flourishing cliffside garden at "Draughts", West Bumpkettle. LORD GRAPPLINGHOOKS - AWASH is wearing the elastic harness which enables him to cultivate his 3 acre garden several hours at a stretch. "A cliff garden is sheer hard work of course" says Lord Grapplinghooks - Awash, who has recently put in a good row of peas by hang glider.

5. FROST POCKET GARDEN IS A CHALLENGE.

On an iceberg in The Antarctic, Robin and Fiona Twittering, a retired couple from Nasal in Hursthumphkinshire survey their budding arpeggio which has taken 15 years to germinate using a method derived from local penguins.

PATIENCE IS REQUIRED   A MOVING MOMENT.

PESTS

- The most effective method of dealing with harmful INSECTS - (including killer bees and African soldier ants) must be our useful friend the CARNIVEROUS PLANT.

ECOLOGICALLY FRIENDLY - A GROVE OF CARNIVEROUS PLANTS

Above: NEAT AND SPEEDY, - NO HARMFUL CHEMICALS, NO MESS, - THE CARNIVEROUS PLANT TAKES CARE OF NOXIOUS INSECT PESTS.

NOTE: CARNIVEROUS PLANTS ARE NOT EFFECTIVE AGAINST THE GIANT SPINACH WEEVIL

BIRDS AND SMALL RODENTS may be discouraged by means of a model PREDATORY EAGLE or ANACONDA. Can be adapted To look up or down depending on which direction The pest is coming from.

FOR DOGS, CATS and LIGHT-FINGERED NEIGHBOURS - the recently introduced REALISTIC SPRINGING TIGER is startlingly effective.

Note: This is not effective against LIVE Tigers (in case these happen To be a pest in your garden). In fact a serious drawback is that in mating time it may even attract them.

SPLENDOUR IN THE GRASS:
THE REALISTIC SPRINGING TIGER LEAVES YOUR GARDEN FREE OF UNWANTED INTRUDERS

FURTHER NOTE: Useful Though the above devices may be, it pays to substitute The real thing occasionally for a day or so, to keep pests on Their toes. HOWEVER, it is advisable in This event To make a note of whether The pest control currently at large in the garden is The REAL or MERELY REALISTIC, - as forgetful gardeners have frequently become victims of Their own devices.

PESTS, (CONTINUED)

 NEIGHBOURS: GIANT SPIDERS evenly distributed round the garden will prevent the incursion of a large number of these pests, particularly the female variety. On their own terrain NEIGHBOURS are easily dealt with by the following methods:

a) THE WEED SEED method, (right) which may if necessary be combined with

 b) THE MOLE METHOD
PLACE a line of well rotted manure along the boundary with your neighbour's property. In no time at all worms will eagerly make for the manure, and after them will hasten hungry MOLES. IMMEDIATELY erect a concrete wall to keep the moles from returning to your garden, making this a mere 6" high (because moles cannot jump) but 45 ft deep (because they can dig.) You should have no more trouble.

IF NEITHER OF THESE METHODS IS EFFECTIVE quick results may be achieved with:

 c) THE LOCUST TREATMENT, otherwise known as 'PANDORA'S BOX' (same principal as the WEED SEED method, but substituting thistle down for FRESH LOCUSTS.)

IF YOUR NEIGHBOUR IS NOT GARDEN PROUD, - OR IF INDEED HE HAS NOT GOT A GARDEN:

d) THE FRIENDLY INVITATION TO A CUP OF HERB (Hemlock) TEA may be resorted to.
NOTE: Remember which cup you have put it in.

SOWING THE SEEDS of DISCORD, - SIMPLE BUT EFFECTIVE, - THE WEED METHOD, USING thistle DOWN (nettle, bindweed or ground elder seed are equally effective) having first ascertained that the wind is in the right direction to send the seeds over into your neighbour's garden and not your own

HEMLOCK TEA. THE DIGESTIVE BISCUIT IS ESSENTIAL TO AVERT SUSPICION.

PICKING   An activity that provides potential for your O.G.A.s

a) For the plucking of <u>EXTRA LOW</u> crops, such as DWARF BEANS, STRAWBERRIES etc., The GRADUAL, or DELAYED ACTION BEAN HARVESTER is a MUST, unless the gardener wishes to get that painful and unsightly condition BEAN NECK (see BEANS).

Consisting of a conveyor belt upon which The picker reclines at ease, The mechanism is moved by Tortoises, who are fitted with little muzzles to prevent them partaking of the BEAN FEAST (But they are given some afterwards so as not to break their spirit.)

RIGHT: PICKING DWARF BEANS IN COMFORT on The Tortoise-powered DELAYED ACTION BEAN HARVESTER

b) EXTRA TALL Things, - such as RUNNER BEANS, HOPS, TREE TOMATOES etc., An ELEPHANT LIFT is The ideal Answer To This conundrum, but do <u>not</u> allow him To pick The beans etc himself or you will not get many.
LIKEWISE do not attempt To use This method when picking MEDLARS (-To which elephants are inordinately partial,) as The lifting device is likely to drop The gardener in order to pick the fruit for himself.

MISS VERRUCA McTOTEMPOLE (above) whose Elephant 'DIMPLE' dropped her from a height of 27 feet while picking MEDLARS.

THE SENSIBLE WAY TO PICK RUNNER BEANS

PICKING (CONTINUED) For TRICKY THINGS, such as GOOSEBERRIES, prickly pears etc. the HEDGEHOG FILTER may be adopted, which consists simply in passing a hedgehog through the fruit laden bush in question:

SIMPLE BUT EFFECTIVE, - THE HEDGEHOG FILTER METHOD OF PICKING GOOSEBERRIES.

PICKING WITHOUT O.G.A.s For those gardeners unfortunate enough to be without ELEPHANT, HEDGEHOG etc, STILTS may be resorted to for extra TALL fruit and vegetables requiring picking.

PICKING COCONUTS ON STILTS:

ABOVE: THE RIGHT WAY ↑

RIGHT: The wrong way, - the picker has overfilled his basket.

FAR RIGHT do not use stilts on quicksand →

PLANT POTS

left: THE FIRST PLANT POT, — the open jaws of a TYRANNASAURUS, — 500,000,000,000, B.C.

right: an illusion of Self-Sufficiency, for the Town dweller

Below: Ceramic HOLY FAMILY Herb group.

Chives

Parsely

thyme

right: welcoming MEDUSA, in stone, at the portals of Hatewell Hall.

below: SITTING PRETTY, — a delightful pot in porcelaine.

below: Esparto grass volcano in kiln fired earthenware.

right: 'speaking with tongues', — a modern piece in moulded concrete.

above: CAST IRON OCEAN LINER, at the home of a retired sea captain.

PLANT POTS (CONTINUED)

A novel and practical idea is The MOBILE PLANT CONTAINER, consisting of an URN, POT or TUB, (not too large please) affixed to the back of a tortoise by special suction pad available at all good garden centres. These charming "FLOWER ARRANGEMENTS" may wander at will round your garden, providing an everchanging scene To delight the eye.

PHEW!

left: do not overload

FROM PETITE PERFECTION...

...To the RHODEDENDRON GROVE (above)

MOBILE LAWN AND BIRD BATH.

NOTE: IT IS NOT ADVISABLE TO ALLOW YOUR TORTOISE PLANT POTS To move IN THE SAME AREA as your other O.G.A.s, as The former will only serve as a mobile canteen for the latter.

above: Try to avoid Trailing plants

QUESTIONS ABOUT GARDENING   Some classic horticultural teasers:

QUESTIONS IN THE HOUSE

left: A Government defeat is narrowly averted when question posed by opposition Member for Bumpkettle, Agatha Gush: —

"HAVE YOU GOT MR GRUB THE GARDENER?" is answered in the negative by the Minister for Horticulture, Orsten Thrips.

Below: A cabinet reshuffle.

GARDENERS' QUESTION TIME

The popular BBC (Bumpkettle Broadcasting Corporation) programme comes to the picturesque village of Droop. Soil 50% Quicksand, 50% permafrost. Your chairman Humphrey Clump, and Team: Rodney Trundlebarrow, Phyllis Twinkle, Dr. Wormwood Blight, and guest speaker, — That well known horticultural HIGH Priestess, — LADY AGRIPPA DEADNETTLE.

left: members of the GARDENERS' QUESTION TIME team successfully parry the interrogative thrusts from sprightly garden enthusiasts at Lower Droop Village Hall.

QUESTION: "What Ho!" (a trick question, — really, — "what hoe?") ANSWER: "Dutch".

QUESTION: "Wych ELM?" (DITTO... really "Which elm?")   ANSWER: "Dutch".

QUESTION: "Is loam friable?"   ANSWER: "Yes, in a little butter, but don't overdo the salt."

QUESTION: "How many slugs can you fit in a telephone box?"

ANSWER: "Not known, because the thought of a telephone box full of slugs is so repulsive, no one has as yet been prevailed upon to count them."

RABBITS
Incursions from these pests are no longer a problem when you acquire a BUNNAPULT (illustrated below).

right, the gardener's boon, the BUNNAPULT in action. Adapted from the ancient device, the catapult, the BUNNAPULT flings ingressing rabbits back over the garden fence keeping them on the move so they haven't got a spare moment to burrow underneath.

FENCE

HOLE

ROCK GARDENS
One of the earliest forms of gardens, developed by STONE AGE MAN for growing mustard and cress.

MUSTARD AND CRESS

STONE AGE MEN CULTIVATING THEIR ROCK GARDENS, in 1008957 BC.

ROOF GARDENS. Practical and

space saving, but there are certain disadvantages of which the roof gardener should be aware:

Watering the roof garden in time of war can present special problems, (right)

← ROOF GARDEN

BESIEGING ARMY.

MOAT →

OUTER RAMPARTS

SMALL HOUSES ON A SLOPE (left) are not suitable subjects for roof gardens.

<u>LEANING TOWERS</u> (below) In these circumstances do not indulge in too much foliage, - remembering always that plants are sensitive to the light.

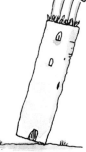

THUMP!

1. MORNING   2. MIDDAY   3 EVENING   4. NIGHT

ROSES

SHALL I COMPARE THEE TO A SUMMER'S DAY?
THY EYES ARE SHADY GROTS. THINE HAIR
A BALE OF HAY,
PIMPERNELS THINE CHEEKS. THINE NOSE
A FULL BLOWN ROSE *

Winton Shaespy

* It is thought his wife suffered from hay fever.

Some rare and unusual roses to grace your garden:

'THE ROSE OF SLOUGH', - Named after the famous heiress
daughter of a Slough butcher, - MISS PUTRID GLOPP, known for her
remarkable complexion, This rose is an undesirable combination of
puce and maroon verging on brownish grey.

'MILDEW' - Named after miss Glopp's younger sister Mildew. This is
an interesting rose covered with distinctive greenish blotches That
turn black with age.

'TOAD IN THE HOLE' - a delightful little rose, - sickly yellow
with a greasy pink centre.

'AMMONIA', - It's certain undefinable perfume will
permeate your garden, drawing gasps from passersby.

'CABBAGE WHITE' - Called 'THE VEGETARIAN'S ROSE'
because it smells of boiled cabbage.

'ANTIQUITY', - One of The true MUST ROSES,
smelling of damp cupboards.

'KEBAB' - also known as 'TORQUEMADA'
this rose's distinctive foliage conceals
impressive thorns two feet long. Flowers
once every 23 years.

THORNS OF THE
REDOUBTABLE ROSE
'KEBAB' A USEFUL
HEDGE.

SEEDS Some interesting facts about seeds:

1. GIANT PODS:

THESE SAVAGES ARE ROWING IN WHAT RESEMBLES A
DUG OUT CANOE BUT IS REALLY THE SEED POD OF A
GIANT AFRICAN HARDWOOD, THE 'LEGGIT TREE'
(so called because that is the sensible thing to do if the
pods start falling.)

2. SEEDS AS WEAPONS:

THIS SEEMINGLY HARMLESS BOUQUET
(right) WAS HANDED TO PRINCE
FRITTER VON FRIEDENGREASE ON THE
FATEFUL FRIDAY 13th AUGUST 1831.
A MOMENT LATER HE LAY DEAD, PEPPERED WITH
147 HOLES MADE BY THE SEEDS OF THE
DEADLY MACHINE GUN PLANT WHOSE PODS
BURST WITH SUCH FORCE THAT THEY ARE IDEAL
FOR POLITICAL MURDERS BY THOSE WHO CARE ABOUT THE ENVIRONMENT.

Ecologically
friendly, -
The seeds of the
MACHINE GUN PLANT

3. COMPLICATED LIFE CYCLE AND SEED DISTRIBUTION:

← Left, the LONG SUFFERING SEED OF THE PATIENCE OF JOB TREE,
WHICH REQUIRES TWO ICE AGES, THREE VOLCANIC ERRUPTIONS,
TEN THOUSAND YEARS IN A SWAMP, AND PASSAGE THROUGH THE
GUT OF A RHESUS NEGATIVE TRICEROTOPS IN ORDER TO GERMINATE.

right, nearly there,
but the Tricerotops was
rhesus positive, so no
germination this time.

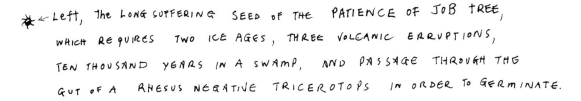

SPECIAL EFFECTS

There is NO EXCUSE for your garden to be boring or ordinary, now that a large selection of SPECIAL EFFECTS is available. The following are particularly imposing:

MOUNTAINS - including EVEREST LOOK-ALIKE

GORGES - CHEDDAR-TYPE And GRAND CANYON PARTICULARLY RECOMMENDED

LAKES - WITH OR WITHOUT WHIRLPOOLS, HOT GEYZERS

And IMITATION NIAGARA FALLS

OR WHY NOT ORDER:

A DESERT - ENTIRELY RUN BY SOLAR ENERGY, - DUST STORMS A DELUXE EXTRA

* A TROPICAL STORM!

* A TIDAL WAVE!

* AN EARTHQUAKE!

* A VOLCANO!

Something to entertain your guests or get rid of them depending on how operated.

WUTHERING HEIGHTS - SIR ED FIRST, 99 YEAR OLD VETERAN OF THE ILL-FATED 1910 BUMPKETTLE EVEREST EXPEDITION, RELIVES ITS THRILLS AND SPILLS ON HIS IMITATION MATTERHORN, PICKED UP AT HALF PRICE IN THE JANUARY SALES.

* ALL SUPPLIED BY DIVINE FORCES
(Not on the phone - may be contacted by prayer.)

From their living room window at "Eldorado" Stan and Winnie EVERCROUCH survey a gathering duststorm in their desert garden. "It saves going on holiday to the Costa Brava" says winnie, whose hobbies are patchwork and making fudge.

SPECIAL EFFECTS (CONTINUED)

A TREAT FOR TRAIN ENTHUSIASTS! For a fairly reasonable sum Bumpkettle Rail will arrange for an INTERCITY EXPRESS to be diverted through your garden. Or, if you are VERY enthusiastic about Trains, your lawn can become a RAILWAY JUNCTION, with 25 Through Trains, or 50 stopping trains per minute.

Not to be outdone, BUMPKETTLE AIRWAYS have come up with a similar offer to Plane Spotters, who can now, at an amazingly low price have INTERNATIONAL JUMBO JETS taking off from their drive. Rocket launching also available by special arrangement.

FOR HISTORICAL TYPES, - Take a trip down Memory Lane, with Genuine FIRST WORLD WAR TRENCHES, - ex-army surplus plus shell holes. Enact it all again in your own back yard! OR for the POLITICALLY AWARE, - it is now possible to HIRE A RALLY to take place right outside your front door.

While for those of a more INDUSTRIAL FRAME of MIND what could be more suitable than a FACTORY in the garden? - Do your bit to boost Bumpkettle Industry, while at the same time deriving intense enjoyment from all those smoking chimneys. OR, more DOWN TO EARTH, - a COAL PIT! or even a COAL TIP! - or both! Your friends will give their eye teeth to have thought of something so original.

Rocket launching in Suburbia, - Gordon and Eva Bargepole watch the 57th launching of Space Shuttle Icarus II "I don't know where we'd be without it," says Eva.

TREE SURGERY

If you notice SOMETHING STIRRING in the Greenwood, it is most likely the TREE SURGEON going about his heroic duties:

TREATMENT FOR A BROKEN LIMB.

PATIENT RECOVERING FROM ROOT SURGERY

A DECISIVE MOMENT FOR THE SURGEON

EXAMINING A SICK TREE, — The tree surgeon's job can be dangerous.

UNSPEAKABLE GARDENS - the following are exceptionally

unpleasant gardens NOT recommended by Bumpkettle Horticultural Society:

left, <u>Snake pit</u> in the garden at "Hissings," home of the late Miss Ethne Warble, missing since July 10th 1987. Far left, Miss Warble's pet anaconda Voodoo Boy, photographed soon after Miss Warble's disappearance.

<u>Tragedy on the Steppes:</u>
The Winter Gardens of Princess Spittina Spittoonovitch and her lover Count Ivan (prop. of the well known 2nd hand furniture shop, IVAN'S DIVANS), showing the unfinished winter palace that was to be their dream cottage in the country. It is thought that the architect employed for the construction harboured a grudge. HAUNTED.

Dolorous domes: quicksands swallow the winter palace of Princess Spittina Spittoonovitch.

Right, <u>From Here To Eternity</u>
Photograph of the garden at Tottering Towers at the moment when it was sucked into a Black Hole on 15th May 1952, as was the owner, Sir Crispin Briskett-Truss, and a young lady visitor, identified only as "Trixie."
Below, right, a pair of braces, and $\frac{1}{2}$ bottle of Chablis that for some inexplicable reason escaped the holocaust.

Below: <u>The Jungle Look</u> - Unidentified South American Creeper overruns the garden of famous gardener and broad caster Rodney Trundlebarrow, after he returned from holiday with an "exciting new variety of Bizzy Lizzy."

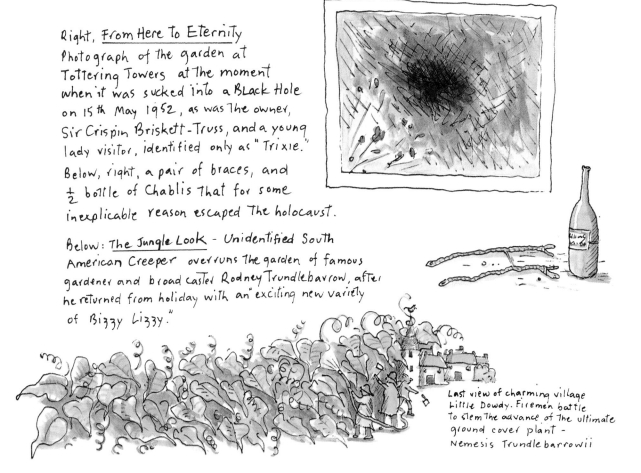

Last view of charming village Little Dowdy. Firemen battle to stem the advance of the ultimate ground cover plant - Nemesis Trundlebarrowii

VINEYARDS

It is not generally known that HANNIBAL produced a very tolerable wine in his vineyard over the other side of the Alps. Known as VIN MAIGRE it was a remarkably thin bodied wine owing to the fact that the grapes were all trampled by Elephants, — as indeed was the whole vineyard.

Did YOU KNOW that the BATTLE OF AGINCOURT was started by GRAPE PIPS? Hannibal's elephants were very fond of making regular incursions into the vineyard for the purpose of scrumping the grapes, afterwards spitting out the pips. The latter on one occasion hit the King of France so hard while out on a picnic nearby that he fell over quite literally 'stoned'. There followed a cursory examination by the Surgeon Royal, who pronounced the cause to be lead shot (now known after this incident as 'grape shot') and an English assassination plot was suspected, with the result that war was declared on England.

A CURSORY EXAMINATION OF THE KING OF FRANCE'S WOUNDS, CAUSED IN REALITY BY HIGH VELOCITY GRAPE PIPS.

WATERING

A careful balance is required in this important aspect of gardening.

1. OVERWATERING   2. UNDERWATERING.

Diverting the nearest river to irrigate your garden can be both costly and laborious (below)

while, on a smaller scale, even the conventional hose pipe can be a headache at times.

left:
TRYING TO FIND THE END OF THE GARDEN HOSE PIPE, — A SCULPTURE FROM ANCIENT GREECE, now in Bumpkettle museum

WATERING (CONTINUED)

.1. THE SIMPLE WAY,

a bucket with a hole in it,
if you've got all day.   →

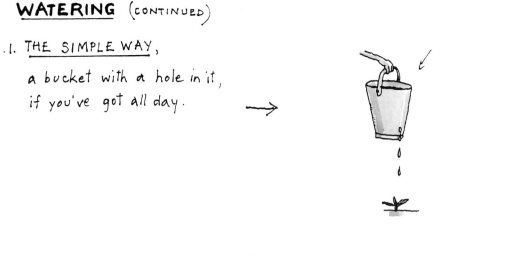

2. WATERING WITH YOUR O.G.A.S

a) BASIC, -
Elephant + RAINBUTT

b) IMPROVED, -
Elephant + Rainbutt on WHEELS

c) AUTOMATIC, -
Elephant + RAINBUTT ATTACHED.

A PAIR OF PACHYODERM STROLLING SPRAYERS.

WEEDS

WEEDS - An area of gardening upon which The gardener can bring his O.G.A. to bear, according to Their suitability for The task. Examples of usefulness in This respect are: doNKEYS, PIGS, ELEPHANTS and LOCUSTS, - if a scorched earth effect is desired.

BELOW: CONTROL of The O.G·A· is essential when weeding between crops.

right: Colonal Smattering of The Royal Horticultural Corps (retired) weeds his kitchen garden at 'Battlefields' with the aid of his giant Irish Bog Slug, Peter.

blinkers

weeds

lettuces

right: for gardeners without O.G.A.s, -

<u>LADY AGRIPPA'S HOMEMADE TOBASCO SAUCE</u> is The recommended remedy for weeds.

FIREBALL TOBASCO SAUCE

ADD TO STEWS AND CURRIES FOR THAT CERTAIN "je ne sais quoi"!

USE AS A WEEDKILLER, TO ELIMINATE: VIPERWEED GALLOPING GOUTFOOT, SLOUCH FRIZZLE, RABID RETCH MEANDER, BLUE FUNK HYENA'S BREATH, GAMP, GROPE, VULTURE'S CLAW & MY LADY'S BUNION.

NOTE: DO NOT USE AS AN ANTI-DANDRUFF SHAMPOO. MAY CAUSE BLISTERS, LOSS OF MEMORY OR FOAMING AT THE MOUTH

left: SILENT AND DEADLY, - LADY AGRIPPA'S HOMEMADE TOBASCO SAUCE, KNOWN AS 'THE WEEDS' WATERLOO.' JUST ONE APPLICATION WILL MAKE THOSE WEEDS SHOOT BACK INTO THE GROUND

Note: Can also be used as a cure for ingrowing Toenails in Elephants.

WHEELBARROWS

The WHEELBARROW throughout history:

STONE AGE WHEELBARROW

CARVED FROM A SINGLE BOULDER BY DEER ANTLER
THIS WHEELBARROW WAS PARTICULARLY HARD TO
PUSH ALONG SINCE THE INVENTION OF THE
WHEEL HAD NOT YET TAKEN PLACE.

WATTLE AND DAUB
WHEELBARROW –
A FINE EXAMPLE OF
EARLY ENGLISH
CRAFTSMANSHIP

HOLLOWED
OUT
TREE TRUNK

WOOD AGE WHEELBARROW

17th CENTURY SELF PROPELLING
WHEELBARROW – AN EARLY EXAMPLE
OF THE RATCHET PRINCIPLE.

BOADICEA'S WHEELBARROW
with the added advantage
that it cut the verges and
enemies' legs at the same time.

IRON AGE WHEELBARROW –
A MAGNIFICENT SPECIMEN MADE
BY THE FAMOUS GERMAN CRAFTSMAN
B. GUNTER RUSTE.

FRENCH
MAID

ROMAN WHEELBARROW
WITH DUNG SPREADING
ATTACHMENT.

cut
here

LOUIS VXTH WHEELBARROW.
TORTOISESHELL INLAID WITH MOTHER OF PEARL
SAID TO HAVE BEEN USED AS A SHOPPING TROLLEY
BY MADAME de POMME de TERRE.

WORMS Well known to the gardener as the animated pink elastic tube that moves silently among the sods in its quest for humus. Interestingly, one of the famous PLAGUES of EGYPT was an epidemic of GIANT WORMS, which attracted GIANT MOLES. These in their turn became a severe problem, covering the land with enormous MOLE HILLS. Fossilised remains of the latter are still to be found in Egypt today. Known as PYRAMIDS, they are a sober reminder of the horticultural catastrophes that can befall the ungodly gardener.

← worm

right: GIANT EGYPTIAN WORMS FLEE FROM GIANT EGYPTIAN MOLE.

THE DIET OF WORMS. Mention of this phenomenon appears in an early report by the Bikings or 'Vikings' on their tour of Europe, who on arriving in Italy wrote home that the natives ' looke surprysynglie fitte onne a Diette of Wormes," an early reference, of course, to the Italian national dish,— spaghetti.

Above · the Bikings did not care for the Italian national dish, spaghetti.

eXERCISE IN THE GARDEN

From earliest times GARDENS have been the scene of vigorous sporting activities:

REMAINS OF FOSSILIZED WOODLOUSE, USED IN THE EARLIEST GARDEN SPORT,- WOODLOUSE RACING, PRACTISED BY EARLY MAN.

above:
STONEHENGE, - The first CROQUET LAWN where The Traditional game 'SLAB CROQUET' was played, with The added excitement That The players never knew when they would be crushed by Toppling stones.

HUNTING was popular with The Romans, who amused themselves chasing wild boars, Tigers and other dangerous beasts round a maze specially grown for The purpose, - until it occurred to the Emperor Nero that it would be considerably more entertaining to make The boars, tigers etc. chase The Romans. So every now and Then he would give a signal, (three notes on his violin) and the proceedings were reversed.

FRAGMENT OF A VIOLIN, THOUGHT TO HAVE BELONGED TO The EMPEROR NERO. NOW IN BUMPKETTLE MUSEUM

The game of BOWLS, so popular with Drake, originated in Hannibal's time, when it was known as 'BOWELS' and played with The ubiquitous balls of fresh elephant dung.

AN APPEAL to players of LAWN GOLF : PLEASE ALways ensure That The course is cleared of HEDGEHOGS.

HANNIBAL and friend playing BOWELS, or 'BOWLS' as it is now called.

left: this is one reason why SWISS HEDGEHOG CHEESE is now so rare.

YE OLDE BYGONES

Lady Agrippa's famous collection of Bygones dug up by gardeners, and now housed in Bumpkettle Museum. Notable for its ALPINE CHEESE PRESS for HEDGEHOG CHEESE, - (fromage piquante). The collection also includes a set of milking thimbles worn for milking hedgehogs, - a souvenir picked up by Hannibal on his journey over the Alps.

EARLY ENGLISH CUSTARD CREAMS in ORIGINAL BISCUIT TIN, RECENTLY UNEARTHED, NOW in BUMPKETTLE MUSEUM.

LEFT: a RARE DEVICE FOR KNOCKING RIPE GRAPES OFF THE VINES THUS LEAVING ONLY THE SOUR ONES WHICH WERE THEN PICKED AND MADE INTO THE TRADITIONAL LOCAL DELICACY, - 'BUMPKETTLE BILGE', — (an acquired taste.)

SET OF SWISS MILKING THIMBLES WORN FOR MILKING HEDGEHOGS.

HANDLE, MADE FROM TUSK OF A STEGASAURUS

EARLY CASTORS.

REMAINS OF FIRE

LEFT,: STONE AGE COOKER, STILL IN REMARKABLE CONDITION, COMPLETE WITH ½ MAMMOTH, WHICH HAS BECOME FOSSILISED IN THE PROCESS OF COOKING. (THIS IS NOT SURPRISING BECAUSE THE PROCESS TOOK A GOOD MANY YEARS ON THIS PRIMITIVE STOVE.)

ABOVE: ANCIENT CORINTHIAN PLOUGHING SHOE, WORN BY WOMEN.

ZEPPELIN GARDENS

The GARDEN OF THE FUTURE, The AIRSHIP or 'ZEPPELIN' GARDEN is the answer to crowded city dwelling.

SKIES OVER BUMPKETTLE: 'NOT A YARD OF GROUND TO SPARE SO HAVE YOUR GARDEN IN THE AIR' — THE SOLUTION TO THE HOUSING SHORTAGE. - A scheme TO DEVELOP THE GREEN BELT AND PUT parks, GARDENS, bits of countryside etc on a higher plane.

TRANSPARENT

right: IN HIS TETHERED ZEPPELIN GARDEN, REGINALD TEABAG TENDS HIS VINUS VULGARIS, WHILE HIS WIFE PRUNE DESCENDS TO 'PUSSY WILLOWS' TO PUT ON THE DINNER. ABOVE THEM LOBELIA CATCHFLY WAFTS PAST IN HER AIRBORNE SMALLHOLDING WITH HER PEDIGREE COW DOLLOP, AND TWINS PHLOX AND FUSCHIA.